Journey of a Glass of Milk

John Malam

www.raintreepublishers.co.uk
Visit our website to find out more information about Raintree books.

To order:
☎ Phone 0845 6044371
🖷 Fax +44 (0) 1865 312263
🖳 Email myorders@raintreepublishers.co.uk

Customers from outside the UK please telephone +44 1865 312262

Raintree is an imprint of Capstone Global Library Limited, a company incorporated in England and Wales having its registered office at 7 Pilgrim Street, London, EC4V 6LB – Registered company number: 6695582

Edited by Dan Nunn and Diyan Leake
Designed by Cynthia Della-Rovere
Original illustrations © Capstone Global Library Ltd 2012
Illustrated by Capstone Global Library Ltd
Picture research by Mica Brancic
Production by Alison Parsons
Originated by Capstone Global Library Ltd
Printed and bound in China by Leo Paper Products Ltd

ISBN 978 1 406 23935 5 (hardback)
16 15 14 13 12
10 9 8 7 6 5 4 3 2 1

British Library Cataloguing in Publication Data
Malam, John, 1957-
   Journey of a glass of milk.
   641.3'71-dc22
A full catalogue record for this book is available from the British Library.

Acknowledgements
The author and publishers are grateful to the following for permission to reproduce copyright material: Alamy pp. 4 (© David Page), 13 (© Photofusion Picture Library), 14 (© Norman West), 18 (© Leslie Garland Picture Library), 19 (© Nigel Cattlin), 22 (Flatbread Images, LLC/© Thom Gourley), 23 (© pixel shepherd), 25 (© Christine Whitehead), 26 (© Art Directors & TRIP); Corbis pp. 11 (© Helen King), 27, 28 (© moodboard); Science Photo Library p. 24 (James King-Holmes); Shutterstock pp. title page (© Sandra Gligorijevic), 5 (Dmitriy Shironosov), 6 (Kevin Day), 7 (© EcoPrint), 8 (© holbox), 9 (© Nancy Gill), 10 (© bioraven), 12 (© Mark Yuill), 17 main (© zirconicusso), 20 (© Lucky_Li), 29 top (© holbox), 29 bottom (© zirconicusso), 31 top (© bioraven), 31 bottom (© Sandra Gligorijevic); © Tetra Pak p. 21 (Lamination Department, Lund, Sweden); © Yeo Valley pp. 15, 16 & 31 middle.

Cover photographs of a glass of milk and cow hide reproduced with permission of © Shutterstock.

Every effort has been made to contact copyright holders of material reproduced in this book. Any omissions will be rectified in subsequent printings if notice is given to the publisher.

641·371

Contents

Some words are shown in bold, **like this**. You can find out what they mean by looking in the Glossary.

What is milk?

Milk is a liquid made in the bodies of adult **female mammals** such as humans, cows, goats, sheep, and reindeer. They feed it to their young to help them grow and protect them from disease.

This mother goat is feeding milk to her kid.

Lots of people like to drink cows' milk.

Milk has **calcium** in it. This can help you grow healthy teeth and bones. Have you ever wondered about the journey milk takes to get from a cow to you? Read on to find out!

Dairy cows

A cow has her first calf when she is about two years old. She starts to **produce** milk after this. A cow that produces milk is called a **dairy cow**.

A calf is a baby cow.

These dairy cows are called Friesians.

Farmers keep **herds** of dairy cows for their milk. Small herds have just a few cows. Bigger herds have more than 100 cows. There are many **breeds** of dairy cow. Some breeds produce more milk than others.

Eat, eat, eat!

Dairy cows are hungry animals. An adult cow eats about 45 kilograms (100 pounds) of food every day. A cow spends around eight hours a day eating and drinking. In summer, cows mainly eat **fresh** grass in the fields.

Cows spend a long time chewing their food.

These cows are being fed in winter.

In winter, cows stay indoors. Farmers keep grass in a special way to feed their cows in winter. This grass is called silage. Cows drink lots of fresh water every day, all year round.

Making milk

udder

A **dairy cow** stores milk in her **udder**. The udder looks like a bag underneath the cow, near her back legs. A cow makes about 30 litres of milk every day. That's a lot of milk!

Farmers usually milk their cows twice a day, morning and evening. The cows walk to the milking **parlour**, where milking machines suck the milk from their udders. It takes about 5 to 8 minutes to milk a cow. Then the cows walk back to the field or barn.

This farmer is using a machine to milk his cows.

Collecting the milk

The farmer stores the **raw milk** in a big metal tank on the farm. The tank is as cold as a fridge, to keep the milk **fresh**.

The metal tank stores a lot of milk.

Milk flows along a pipe into the tanker lorry.

Every day, a tanker lorry gets the raw milk from the farm. It drives around and collects milk from several farms. The lorry takes the milk to the **dairy** when it is full.

At the dairy

The **dairy** is where **raw milk** from cows is **processed** into drinking milk for humans. The raw milk is pumped out of the tanker lorry and into the dairy's storage tanks.

Tanker lorries take milk to the dairy every day.

The raw milk is pumped into a **pasteurization** machine. The machine heats the milk up until it is very hot. Then it cools the milk down very quickly. This process kills any harmful **bacteria**. It makes the milk safe to drink.

Mixing in the cream

A layer of cream floats to the top of **raw milk** that is left to stand still. The milk is **homogenized** to stop this. This means it is forced through lots of very thin tubes.

Raw milk is squeezed through tubes.

The cream is spread evenly through this glass of milk.

As the milk is squeezed along the tubes, the cream spreads evenly through it. When the milk stands still now, the cream will not float to the top.

Milk bottles and cartons

The milk may be put into a plastic or a glass bottle. It may be put into a cardboard carton.

These are glass bottles being filled with milk.

These plastic bottles are full of milk.

Today, most milk is put into plastic bottles and cardboard cartons. The milk in bottles and cartons is measured in pints or litres.

Cardboard milk cartons

Milk cartons are made from thin cardboard. The cardboard is covered inside with a very thin layer of plastic called **polythene**. This stops the milk from leaking out.

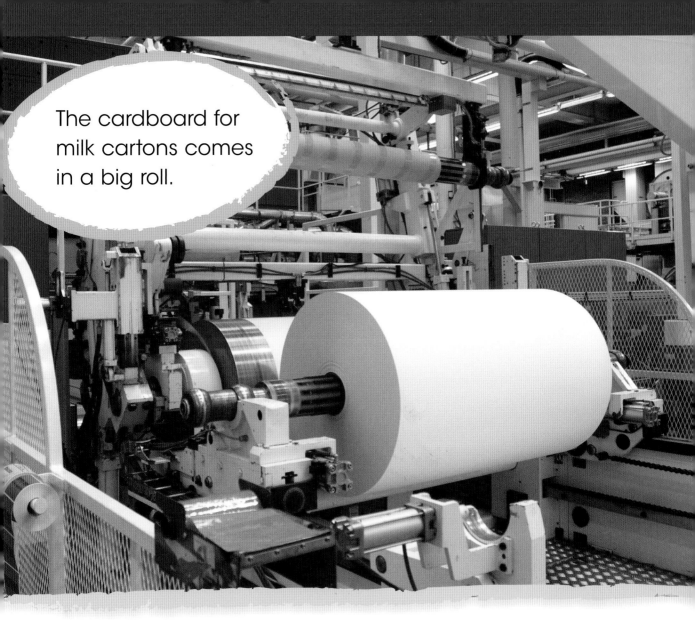

The cardboard for milk cartons comes in a big roll.

New milk cartons are flat when they come to the **dairy**. A machine folds them into cartons and fills them with milk.

Plastic milk bottles

Have you noticed the letters HDPE on a plastic milk bottle? They are usually quite small and close to the **recycling** symbol. They stand for high density polyethylene. This is the type of plastic used to make the bottle.

Look for the letters HDPE on a plastic milk bottle.

You can see the milk in a bottle made of HDPE.

HDPE is a good plastic for milk bottles. It can be made into a bottle that fits into most fridge doors. It is **translucent**. This means you can see how much milk is in the bottle.

Filling with milk

Milk is put into milk bottles and cartons at the **dairy**. It happens after the cream has been mixed into the milk. Milk travels through pipes to a filling machine.

These plastic bottles are being filled with milk.

Best Before:

04 APR 11 B

This milk was best used before 4 April 2011.

Bottles and cartons line up underneath the filling machine. Milk is poured into them. The bottles and cartons are sealed when they are full. A date is stamped on to them. It shows how long the milk will stay **fresh**.

At the shops

Lorries take the bottles and cartons of milk from the **dairy** to shops and supermarkets. The lorries are refrigerated. This keeps the milk cool for the journey.

This milk is being delivered to a shop.

Shoppers choose the milk they want.

People working at the shops put the bottles and cartons on to shelves. The shelves are as cool as a fridge. This keeps the milk **fresh**.

Milk, please!

Customers buy the milk and take it home. The shop pays the **dairy** that **processed** and bottled the milk. The dairy pays the farmer whose cows **produced** the **raw milk**.

People like to drink milk.

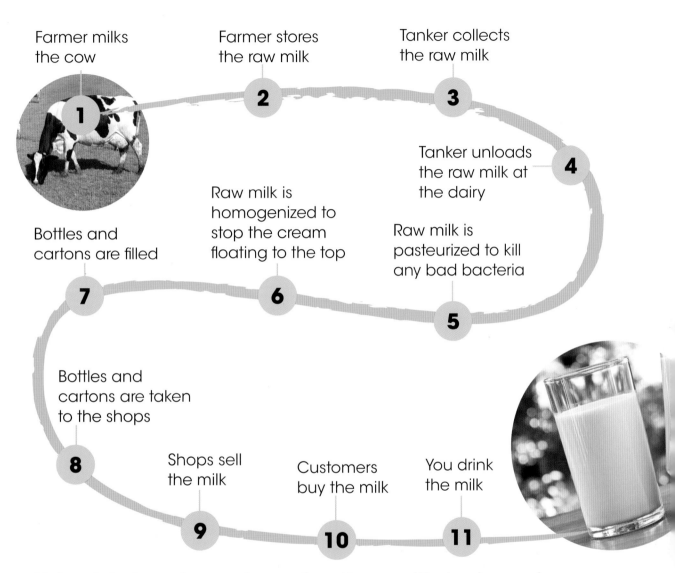

Farmer milks
the cow

1

Farmer stores
the raw milk

2

Tanker collects
the raw milk

3

Tanker unloads
the raw milk at
the dairy

4

Raw milk is
homogenized to
stop the cream
floating to the top

6

Raw milk is
pasteurized to kill
any bad bacteria

5

Bottles and
cartons are filled

7

Bottles and
cartons are taken
to the shops

8

Shops sell
the milk

9

Customers
buy the milk

10

You drink
the milk

11

It just takes two days for the milk to travel
from a cow to your glass. It's amazing to
think that the milk you drink today came
from a farm just two days ago!

Glossary

bacteria very small living things

breed one kind of an animal

calcium chemical that is part of bones and teeth

dairy building where milk is processed ready for use

dairy cow cow that produces milk

female animal that can be a mother

fresh something that is newly made

herd group of cows

homogenize mix raw milk to stop the cream floating to the top

mammal animal where the female gives birth to live young and feeds them on milk from its body

parlour place where cows are milked

pasteurization heating and cooling milk quickly to kill any harmful bacteria

polythene a type of thin plastic

process prepare for use

produce make

raw milk milk that comes straight from the cow

recycling saving things so that they can be used again. They may be used as they are, or made into a new material.

translucent see-through but not totally clear

udder part of a cow from where the milk comes

Milk quiz

1. What is a cow who gives milk called? (see page 6)

2. What is the part of a cow from where the milk comes? (see page 10)

3. What does pasteurization kill? (see page 15)

4. What floats to the top of raw milk? (see page 16)

5. Where is milk put into bottles and cartons? (see page 24)

Find out more

Milk it for all it's worth – a website with information, videos, games, and competitions about milk: **www.milkitforallitsworth. co.uk/#/home**

Download a PowerPoint presentation or a video from this website for the story of a school visit to a dairy farm: **www. foodafactoflife.org.uk/Sheet.aspx?siteId=14&sectionId=100& contentId=434**

Answers

1. dairy cow, 2. the udder, 3. bacteria that are harmful, 4. cream, 5. at a dairy

Index